MENTAL EXERCISES

Torkom Saraydarian

T.S.G. PUBLISHING FOUNDATION, INC.

Mental Exercises

ISBN: 0-929874-53-6

Library of Congress Catalog Card Number: 96-60650

Printed in the United States of America

Printed by: *KNI Incorporated*
               Anaheim, California

Published by: **T.S.G. Publishing Foundation, Inc.**
               P.O. Box 7068
               Cave Creek, AZ 85331-7068
               U.S.A.

All meditations and visualizations are given as guidelines. They
should be used with discretion and after receiving professional
advice. This book is a transcription of a seminar given by Torkom
Saraydarian.

Table of Contents

CHAPTER ONE

The Three Powers
of the Soul

We are going to do lots of exercises today. Some people think that when they read and they listen, they are doing all that is possible to transform their nature. This is not really true. Reading helps, listening helps, but these also create lots of responsibilities and pressure within our system because to read and to listen means to accumulate lots of information, knowledge — energy, in other words. If these energies are not assimilated and transformed and do not become an actuality in our life, it creates lots of responsibility for us. There is no meaning in accumulating them without the intention or possibility to use them.

What we are going to do today is to lessen the pressure that you have accumulated around yourself — the knowledge, the information, lots of truths or falsehoods in your aura. Whatever you learn, whatever you listen to goes into the bag we call your aura. Your aura is a bag. Sometimes it is a trash bag. Sometimes it is a good bag. Sometimes it is also a bank.

This pressure, the accumulation in our aura, must be slowly assimilated and turned into actualization in our life. We cannot actualize them sometimes, but at least we put them into the process of actualization. Sometimes you think to do something and you do it ten years later or fifty years later. This is an example of how you put the energy into process. The energy works, slowly, slowly, conquering the hindrances on the way and assimilating new elements so that, in due time, it actualizes itself.

The exercises we are going to do can be useful to you according to the level of your consciousness, the level of your ability to do them. No matter in what percentage you do them, it is beneficial. Some people will really do them and benefit one hundred percent. Some people will do them five percent and benefit five percent, but in the future they can use that five percent to reach to one hundred percent.

The second thought is that all our civilization is built through our thinking. Civilization is equal to thinking. There is no civilization without thinking. All your bodies: physical, emotional, and mental; all your environment is the result of your thinking. If you read the *Buddha Sutra*, you know how I explained there that man is the result, is the effect of his thinking. His thinking even regulates or conditions his relationships with other people and Nature. Thinking is very important.

The human soul has three very important powers that he uses. **The first power is thinking.** Thinking is one of the powers of the soul. Thinking is the formulation of energies, inspirations, Intuition, and ideas. For example, you go and take a piece of material and that material is equal to inspirations, impressions, and ideas. You cut that material and make a shirt. Making the shirt is thinking. Thinking is formulation — giving shape and form, and adapting the massive amount of material which is inspiration, impressions, and ideas into something that you can use in your daily life and thus build communication lines between you and the Universe. That is what each thought is.

So, every time you think, you take material that is universal, homogeneous. For example, ideas, impressions, inspirations are homogeneous. They do not have forms. You turn them into forms by thinking, and each thought, each form, each thoughtform becomes a contact point between you and other people, between you and the Universe. You must know how to think, and when you think, you will see that thinking creates relationship. You find an ocean and you take a bucket of water and boil it and make it drinkable. That is what the thinking process is: formulation, adaptation to life of things that are homogeneous.

Thinking is very important and we are going to exercise thinking through meditation, through concentration, through our business, through our schooling, university, college, and so on. All these processes and life processes, when making you meet difficulties and hindrances, make you think. All of life is stimulating us or confronting us to make us think. You have a sickness — sickness even is an opportunity to make you think. A problem comes; that problem makes you think. The whole of life, all our relationships, tensions, problems, likes and dislikes, pain and suffering, economical conditions, political conditions — whatever is happening in the world, if you are not dead, makes you start thinking why and how these things are happening. Slowly life stimulates you to think, or else you cannot survive. So we can say also that thinking is a means of survival. In the future world the better you think, the better off you will be. The victory of the future world will be the victory of your thinking.

I am just trying to put out a few ideas; I am not going to talk about the entire mystery of thinking. It is a very, very big subject, and I have already written one thousand pages on it.

Consider this question, for example: What is a business? The real business of a business is thinking. A big corporation is becoming good; another is becoming better. Why? It is because they have better thinkers. Thinkers see opportunities and how to link things together so that they make a better business. I am just throwing out little ideas so that you think about them. If your business is going bad, it means you must overcome with better thinking. The better you think, the better will be your business.

The better you think, the better you are; and the better you think, the better your soul expresses itself and the closer it comes to your personality.

Thinking is the first power of the soul. **The second power of the soul is creative imagination.** Creative imagination is the dramatization of the thoughts.

First there is dramatization of the thoughts. For example, you see a lady fall in love with a man and later the man kills her and it is finished. This is a dramatization of a thought. The dramatization becomes a movie. You put millions of things in it and make a three hour movie. That is the dramatization of a thought, of an event. An event is an actualization of a thought. Whatever you think in your heart, that you are going to be.

So the second power of the soul we see is creative imagination, but this is not mere imagination. Psychologists, psychiatrists, and philosophers have messed things up. They do not know what daydreaming is, what imagination is, what creative imagination is, what visualization is. It is chaos.

Creative imagination is the dramatization of events which are the results of our thoughtforms. Having creative imagination means that you become a genius, you become a great artist, a great musician because you know how to dramatize thought and events. For example, I was visualizing and thinking about the Grand Canyon. I wanted to use my creative imagination to put the Grand Canyon into music. That is what creative imagination is. Have you heard that music on the *Infinity* tape?

For example, you take something — let us say you see a mountain. The dramatization of the mountain can be a fantastic painting. It is not only a mountain. You give different meanings, different psychological, philosophical insight and depth to it, and it becomes a drama through your creative imagination. Creative imagination expands it and connects it with many, many layers of consciousness.

In the Grand Canyon music first I am in awe, then I am seeing the peaks and valleys, then little trees, then I am taking in all of them. Then I am scared, then I am in love, then I am losing myself, then I am seeing the river, and so on. The whole psychology is there. This is an example of creative imagination. You can do the same thing. You see a beautiful girl and then write a big poem, "My love . . . " and so on. You can do anything you want with creative imagination.

The third power of the soul is visualization. Visualization is the usage of energy for self-transformation. Energy follows thought. Energy and thought usage become visualization. Visualization is controlled always by your future expectations and visions. In visualization, vision is materialized and accomplished in your life. Whenever you have vision, that vision becomes tangible through the use of energy and creative imagination.

Thought does not have creative imagination and visualization. Rather, creative imagination has thought and creative imagination. Visualization has thought, creative imagination, and visualization. All three are synthesized in creative visualization.

Creative visualization or visualization is the utilization of high energies — spiritual energies, solar energies, and Cosmic energies — to transform, to transfigure, and to build your future bodies, your future connections, your future events, and your future fields of service. Whatever you visualize is powerful. If it is sincere and real, Nature pours out all its energy for the actualization of your visualization because Nature follows a law that says whenever you make a hole, water falls into it. It is a law. For example, you go to the ocean and you make a little track from the ocean to the sand, and the ocean follows the track. Visualization is just like that. You create forms that Nature fills. In a philosophical way, visualization means to create a vacuum in space so that Nature fills it. If you think about it and use creative imagination, this idea can become a book. That is creative visualization.

Today we are going to use creative visualization or visualization in five stages. From this time on, you are going to do the job and I am going to watch you, because filling your barrel with words and knowledge does not mean anything. You are going to create those conditions in which the energies are going to come and start becoming constructive in your life.

One hour of visualization is equal to thirty hours of reading, just because it is practical. For example, you work very hard for thirty days to make a dinner, but then you eat the dinner in one hour and the eating is very important.

CHAPTER TWO

The Five Energies

The first exercise is going to be about **purification.** There is no

— constructive activity

— success

— progress

— health

— happiness

unless the foundation is pure.

The second exercise is **organization**. You organize new mechanisms, new vehicles, new thoughts, new patterns to use the energies that you are receiving.

In the third exercise there is **radiation**. You radiate these energies so that you are not congested and you do not become a balloon — you just radiate them.

The fourth exercise is **creativity**, the use of these energies for constructive ends.

The fifth exercise is **pressure**. It concerns the reality that you are discovering yourself. These are the things we are going to discuss.

WHAT THESE EXERCISES DO

During these exercises several things happen. The most important thing that happens — and you cannot see it for a while or feel it immediately — is that lots of energies hidden in your lower nature go through a process of sublimation. In your barrel you have lots of unused energies — fuel, oil, lots of ores, and so on. They are all there with their mixed conditions. Visualization refines them, transforms them, transmutes them, sublimates them, and uses them for your higher centers. It is a tremendous psychological healing exercise. The first thing that it does — and this is very beautiful — is that it transforms your nature. The aspects of your nature that are latent and unused, those unused energies come slowly to the higher centers and you put them to use. You use them in your thinking, in your feeling, in your actions, in your relationships, in your creativity.

The second thing that visualization does is to evoke energies from the higher realms, from your soul, from your Solar Angel, from spiritual entities, from the Hierarchy, from Teachers and Masters, from Universes.

Something else happens. You receive new energies and these new energies may create certain conflicts in your mind. For example, the first conflict is this. "I am so beautiful, but I am so ugly at the same time. I want to be so great, but I feel so humiliated — at the same time." Higher energies reveal advanced visions and also they reveal the glory hidden within you. But at the same time, under their light you see all the weaknesses of your personality, and this creates conflict within you. It is both sides of your nature coming out. These kinds of conflict are good because in seeing your lower and higher polarities you create a balance between them, and eventually you become the unchanging one. These are just very little hints because each of them takes a seminar.

You can do these exercises according to your depth, your capacity for pressure, your sincerity. My suggestion is to try. Try to do each exercise better and better, and I think that when we end this session, you will really have learned how to visualize. It is a very easy thing to do. It is a very natural thing. The Tibetan Master says that all the great things that are created in the Universe are the result of visualization. God visualized. Can you imagine that our Planetary Logos visualized to have such an earth with millions of insects, animals, human beings, and all this phenomena? Can you imagine how He saw these things? And when He saw it all, He said, "That is good. Let it be," and it became. Nature immediately responded to the visualization.

That will be your life. Visualization is related to your future and to making your future fantastic. It is not for this life only, not for one life only.

The other day I was reading that it took three hundred years for some Italian cathedrals to be built. For some German fortresses it took four hundred years. Many generations passed, but eventually they were built. That is how you are going to do it. You are going to start building now, and then life after life, or suddenly in this life, you will see the results of your visualization.

CHAPTER THREE

Purification

Exercise 1

Purification of the Physical Body

— Now we are going to start. The very first stage is to become comfortable. Forget your body and chair and become really comfortable. You do not know what great fun you are going to have. Close your eyes and relax your body and feel happy. Be happy.

— Concentrate or focus your consciousness in your head. Withdraw it from your body, emotions, and mind, and bring your consciousness to your head between the eyebrows. You are not in the other places of your body; you are between your eyebrows — even outside, not in the body.

— Now you are going to visualize a waterfall, a fantastic waterfall, anyplace you want. You can even create it if you want. I went to Brazil. I saw the waterfalls. My goodness, they were beautiful.

— Okay, now take off your clothes and enter into the waterfall and feel the water. It is so beautiful. Make it as real as you can. First try to wash your body. See how dirt is coming from your body, dirt and dust and many kinds of elements; the water is cleaning, cleaning, cleaning your hair, your head, your back, your chest, your legs, and everywhere. You are becoming cleaner and cleaner and cleaner. Feel the energy of it. Feel the ions of it. Feel the pressure. Feel the coldness. Make it a little cold so that you feel nice. As you make it more real, you will have more benefit from it. Be there. Do not let your mind wander. Just be under the waterfall. I am going to give you a few minutes. Just stand under the waterfall and clean your back, your hair, your hands, and enjoy it like a little child. This is teaching you both how to visualize and how to benefit from it.

You will sweat a little. That is okay, but make the water a little colder. See what is happening with the drops, the water, and the current; see how fantastic they are. The water is pouring over your nose, your hair, and your hands. It is hitting your shoulders, back, and front and everywhere. Just feel it. You are a child. Lie down and feel it pouring upon you. Turn back. Do anything you want. Just make it real. Now that your are receiving this energy on your body say,

Clean me, O Lord, by Your energy.
Cleanse my body.

— Now in the next step visualize that water is penetrating into all your inner organs, cleansing them. Your brain is open and being cleansed, your heart is open, your lungs are open. You are showering inside, outside. Open your mouth. Let it go there. Your stomach is being washed, your intestines are being washed. You have never had a washing like this!

— Now your urination system is being washed, your womb and intestines, now your eyes, your nose, your sinuses, your ears. Energy follows thought. You are releasing lots of energy into your system and purifying it — your lungs, your inner muscles, your bones, your pancreas, your liver. The water is penetrating everywhere. Everything is becoming clean. Microbes, germs, viruses are being flushed out.

— Extend your hands and in your imagination see how the water is coming through your fingers and toes and out from your nose, from your eyes, from your mouth. You are taking a real shower. Say,

Lord,
cleanse me from the afflictions of my body.

— Everything that is dirty, flush it out: germs, microbes, viruses. Take a nice shower inside and outside.

— Do not give up. Just make it more and more real. This is a group therapy. Look and see how water is coming from your ears and cleansing everything. Wherever you have a problem, see water coming out from it. Your eyes are getting washed from inside, from outside; your brain is getting washed because water is electrical energy. It is oxygen and hydrogen which is fire. It is a fire, a liquid fire.

— Now play there, jump and shout. Be happy. As real as you make it, to that degree you benefit from it. Wash your spine, inside, outside, so that when you come out, "Wow," we'll say, "what a beauty." Expose yourself one hundred percent to the water with the intention that you are in the process of purification, total purification.

— Now open your mouth and drink and drink and drink the water and then eliminate it, purer each time. You are overhauling yourself. Next concentrate on your ears, on how water is going out of your ears as out of a hose. You need lots of cleansing in your ears. See how dirt is coming out, pus is coming out, some bugs are coming out, dust is coming out.

— Now do the same thing with your eyes. Your eyes are just like two big holes with water gushing out.

— Take your nose now; the water is pouring out. All the dirt is coming out of your nose. Filthy things are coming out, cleaning out all your sinuses.

— Again your mouth. Open your mouth and let the water come toward your head; let it pour in and then go out from your mouth. All the rest of the dirt is coming out. Visualize well.

— Now visualize that water is pouring through your hands and fingers, ten fingers. Make it fun — pretend that all your fingers are hoses. This cleans all your meridians. Now do the same thing with your toes. Water is cleaning all those magnetic lines.

— Now close your ears, eyes, nose, mouth, toes, and fingers. Let the water come in and make you swell and swell and then let it pour out from the pores of your skin. All over your skin water is just pouring out. It is fantastic.

— Each one of your hairs is like a hose. Let the hoses pour forth. You are like a barrel that has millions of holes. The pores of your skin are letting water pour out everywhere. Now check your body from A to Z. Be sure water is pouring out. Check your body. If any place is not pouring forth, bring the water there and let it pour — nose, ears, eyes, and so on. Let it pour out now from your hair, from your face, back of your face, your neck like a sprinkler. From your whole back now see the water shooting out a hundred meters or more. From your chest now, from your lower body; and now from your knees, from your feet and from your arms — see it pouring out. Now see how from every side of your body water is pouring out. Check and see if it is true, that every part of your body is pouring out water. At first it looks a little dirty, but then it gets cleaner and cleaner and cleaner. Do it until you feel that pure water is coming.

Fantastic!

— Now slowly come out of the waterfall and sit on a rock and start playing with the water with your feet. See how beautiful everything is and how a little deer is looking at you and asking, "What is this man doing?" Suddenly see the deer entering into the waterfall and doing exactly what you did.

— Rub your hands together. Imagine where you are sitting and open your eyes.

This is a million-dollar exercise. If you do this twice weekly, you will see what will happen. It will be good for you.

Exercise 2

Purification of the Astral Body
Part One

— Close your eyes and relax again. These are very, very fantastic exercises. There are no side effects, nothing. They are fantastic — constructive, creative, transformative. Relax your neck. Some of your necks are tense. Let your shoulders go. Just relax. The more you are relaxed, the more you can benefit from the exercise. Tension in your muscles prevents right visualization. All of your body must be totally relaxed.

— Now visualize another waterfall or the same waterfall. When you have approached the waterfall, lie down. You are not in the waterfall, but very close to it, ten feet away maybe. Lie down. You are totally naked. Then leave your physical body there and in your astral body enter into the waterfall. The astral body is just like your physical body, but it looks very silvery and transparent. You can see on your astral body lots of spots, black spots, dirty spots, dark patches. They are called **anger, fear, hatred, jealousy, revenge, slander, malice**. All these patches are like blacktop impressed on your astral body.

— Now you are going to name these patches. For example, you are going to say, "This is **anger**; this is **jealousy**; this is **fear**; this is **hatred**." Now you see how the waterfall is cleaning them, slowly, slowly. First name them. Look to see where they are. This is a very scientific process, and you will see that lots of patches are not being cleaned. They are like blacktop stuck to your astral body — because they are entities. Your effort will be to clean them. — Within your astral body, under the waterfall, think that the water is love energy. You are standing under a shower of love energy, compassion energy, the best purifying and healing agent in the world. Take your time and clean yourself. Sometimes look at your physical body and how it is lying there like a dead body, so that you make it real. Start with your **fear**. See if it is clearing. Make this a heavy waterfall. Let it hit wherever patches are. It can be near your head, it can be many other places. These dark emotions appear exactly as black patches in your astral body, but don't worry — you will be able eventually to clean them.

— Now you are working on the **fear**. Clean the **fear**, wherever the spot, the black patch is. Maybe it is thin and wavy like a snake; maybe it is extended all over. Wash it! Now wash the **anger**. They are not going to be washed away altogether, but the blackness will disappear a little. Now the hatred — the more you purify yourself from hatred, the healthier will be your emotional body and physical body.

— Now take the **jealousy**. It is a little yellow-colored, yellowish with dirty black in it. It can be close to your solar plexus, close to your heart center. It can be on your shoulders, on your breasts. Work very hard to clean that yellowish dirt.

— Now see **revenge**, another spot somewhere. See the **malice**. Now look at your whole astral body, spotted with many black elements. Stand in the water and let the water pour strongly until everything slowly, slowly melts away. Try to cooperate with that "love-fall" so that it cleans you. If you see that something is resisting and does not want to be cleaned, put all your attention there to clean it, whatever it is. Water is fire and God is in the fire.

— We are paying attention to six things: **fear, anger, hatred, jealousy, revenge**, and **malice**. Look to see which one is melting away and which one is resisting, and wherever one is resisting, concentrate the waterfall there. This will treat your physical sicknesses which are the result of the sicknesses of your astral body. Now concentrate on your astral head. Clean it of all these six things. If there are still spots, concentrate on your shoulders, arms, and hands. Clean every spot that is ugly-duckly, malicious, polluted. This is the opportunity to clean it.

— Now go to your chest area; clean your astral chest. Give your physical body a look lying over there, so that you do not identify with it, and now see how you have a silvery-colored, transparent astral body.

— Continue with your chest now. Concentrate there, with the whole waterfall falling upon your chest. If there are spots there, clean them as much as you can. Now go to your abdomen. Lie on your back in your astral body and let the waterfall hit it, millions of drops in one second. Now let it hit your legs — now your thighs, calves, feet.

— See your astral bowels, transparent; then your knees, transparent. Look to see if there are spots there. Usually whenever you have problems in your physical body, you will see spots at the same place in the astral body. Now lie on your stomach. Let the waterfall hit all over your back and clean every portion of it; start to see that some patches of blackness are fading away. Because you do not have a body, you are weightless, so now go up and down in the waterfall in your astral body. You are weightless. You do not have a dense body — it is lying over there. Expose your astral body, inside, outside, to the waterfall. This is not a joke. This is a very important living exercise.

— Now check your astral body to see if there is any place that still is not clean from **fear, anger, hatred, jealousy, revenge, slander**, and **malice**. Wherever there are still patches, try to clear them away with your hands. Rub them, and if they do not rub away, cut that area out and throw it away and then see the astral body filling that cut. That is spiritual surgery. In a few minutes you must feel that you are purifying or cleansing yourself.

— Check your astral body again, starting from your legs. See if you have any dirty patch on your astral legs because if you have any patch, it is the source of your future sickness. Astral sickness takes eight, nine years to come to the physical. Now look at your lower abdomen. Just make your consciousness think that you have an astral body, that you are in the astral body now. You are not the physical body. Make your focus of mind clear because you may fall back to your physical body. Keep thinking that you are functioning astrally now. Looking at your lower abdomen, see if there are any spots there. Expose it to the waterfall. Now go to the middle abdomen. See if you can see spots there. Try to clean them. Go again to the chest area, to your astral ribs, and now the whole chest. See your astral body as pure light, transparent silver.

— Now go to the neck, face, forehead. See if there are any spots there. Some of you can see spots. Check the top of your head. Now look at the back of your head. If there are any spots there, clean them. Look at your shoulders from the back, and then up and down your spine and all around it. Make it clear, real clear, crystal clear. Now look at your back — your seat must be clear, clear, pure. Look at the back of your legs; see them all purified, clean.

— Now check your astral body again and see where the spots are that still need cleaning. Concentrate the water there until you feel that you took a little cleansing shower. Now go to your physical body and see what it is doing on the sand. Notice that your body is pretty hot and messy with sand. Enter into your body, rub your hands together, and remember where you are. Open your eyes.

It is deplorable that until now the majority of humanity cannot use their separate bodies; one as a carriage, for example; one as a boat — the astral body; one as an airplane — the mental body. These are our vehicles, literally, but it takes time, a little exercise, until our brain consciousness gets used to it. Once you are used to it, you will go, for example, in one minute's meditation to your astral body, clean the depression there in one second, and come back. Depression is a dirty patch in your astral body. Your astral body sends the poison to your physical body, and your physical body becomes sick. Sometimes, when the microbes are astral, the doctor cannot do anything because they keep on coming into the physical body. **The astral body is the source of ninety percent of our sicknesses.**

Q & A

Question: Are you to become your astral body or just observe it?

Answer: You are to become it. We are not talking about imagination. As you have a physical body, you have an astral body. You put the physical body aside and now you are acting through your astral body.

For those who did not clean completely, we are going to go back again to do this so that in ten or fifteen minutes we try to clean as much as we can. This time you are going to do it more seriously because this is a great chance to get rid of the astral mess that you have. Let us say there are six kinds of spots still, but instead of **malice** you put in **depression**. Now depression can exist in other bodies also. Depression can be physical, emotional, or mental, but it appears in the astral body very significantly, very outstandingly. You can see depression in the astral body. Then it depresses your mind, it depresses your body.

The astral body is so dangerous. In ancient literature the astral body is called the prostitute. In many kinds of literature, even in religious literature, when you read about a prostitute, it means the astral body. It pollutes this lover and pollutes that lover. It is monkeying with both sides. So you are going to clean the prostitute in your astral body. Most of us, all of us, are more or less prostitutes. Do not misunderstand me. I am talking with sincerity about what it means. We are going to clean that from our nature.

Question: What about guilt?

Answer: Of course guilt is there. Every time you do something wrong physically, emotionally, or mentally you impress your body. That is how Christ was able to tell the woman at the well all about herself. When He saw that girl, He asked, "Can I have a little water?" "I cannot give you water," she replied. Then Christ, looking at her said, "I can tell you that you've had five husbands." She was surprised and asked, "How do you know?" He saw in her aura, or in her astral body, five husbands. In your astral body everything is recorded.

Question: Some of the dark spots were like heavy scabs. I had to pull them off, but they had little roots to them. What do you do about the roots?

Answer: Pull the area again. Pull it out. Burn it. Cut it. Throw it away. Get rid of it because now you are going to sense that it is there. If it is there, you must get rid of it by doing these exercises. There is nothing else. Medicine cannot reach your astral body. For every disease or illness that you have in your three bodies, each of the three bodies has the antidote within it. Each has the power to clean itself, but you are going to find out how. Put your body, whichever one it is, into the cleansing process.

Remember this water is not natural water. **It is love, love-water** which is loving you. When the love energy comes to the dirt, it uses love to cleanse it; it unites with the dirt and pulls it out. Love is unity. Water goes along the surface, but love penetrates; it takes the dirt, cleans it, and throws it out.

Exercise 3

Purification of the Astral Body
PART TWO

— Let us start again. It is not easy, but you are saving lots of dollars in the future that would go to the hospitals. Look at your astral body. Go into your astral body. Go to the waterfall. Imagine that you are taking your astral body. Leave your physical body on the beach. Now look at that physical body. Go play with the leg of your physical body and see if it is like dead. Good — it is dead. Test its hands. Those are dead also. Close its eyes and say, "Stay there." It is like a pair of jeans that you take off and throw in the corner.

— Now you are the astral body. You are a transparent, silvery-like jellyfish, but in the form of a human. You are entering into the waterfall, and the waterfall is love energy. Every drop is love. It is energizing you, purifying you, cleansing you, and, especially, transforming you.

— See the black spots on your body again and let the love energy pour over all your jealousy, revengefulness, hatred, fear, anger, and depression. See them being cleansed away. Turn your body in any direction to see the love waterfall cleaning it. Love-water is pouring on your astral face — feel it, feel how beautiful it is. Clean from your face any dirt that you can imagine. Your astral face is awful. Just clean it because you hide everything in your astral face. Clean it. Make your astral face really shining. Tomorrow you will see that your face is different. I am not joking. Make your face so clean, the astral face, with love energy penetrating every cell in your astral body. Relax the face — your eyelids, your nose, your lips, your ears. Feel the energy hitting you. Do not make it imagination. Just really feel that you are there.

— Pour the love-water into your throat. Your throat is contaminated with millions of stupid things you've said. Cleanse it, your astral throat. Now open your mouth and let your mouth take that energy so that it cleans every dirty thing in your astral mouth. It is transparent.

— Now pour it into your astral ears. There is so much dirt accumulated there from the gossip and slander of people. Clean it. You do not need these things.

— Now clean your nose. Change your position and let the water go to the nostrils; take the water into your nostrils, take it in, and blow it out until you cleanse it. Rinse clean.

— Now do your shoulders.

— Now do your chest again. See if you have any black spots. Work on them. Clean them, wash them. Now see your back, stomach area, arms.

— Clean your arms, because astral arms are a little dirty from doing monkey business.

— Look at your legs, lower abdomen, organs. Clean them totally. Purify them.

— Now stand in the love-water again and take a final shower. Then, go to your physical body and enter in and stand up. Walk around in the water and feel great and say,

"O, my Lord,
I am clean a little."

— Remember where you are. Rub your hands together, rub your face, and slowly open your eyes.

There are many prayers that say, "Cleanse me, O Lord. Cleanse me, O Lord. Cleanse me, O Lord." I would like to work again on these things. We must do this for a whole week so that you overhaul yourself, wash yourself. This is a historical moment for your consciousness that you are getting this opportunity to purify your nature.

You must demonstrate health in all your nature — physically, emotionally, mentally — and people will feel it. They will say, "Wow, what healthy people these are." We wish this for people all over the world — not only for us, but for everybody.

After some of the exercises a few people approached me and said that as they were trying to wash themselves and clean themselves, the black patches were sticking to their hands, their fingers, and so on. This happens. It is a very good sign that you are working on your mess. It is very good. The cleansing takes time. Some people can eliminate their patches in five minutes or half an hour. With other people, because of the extent of the pollution, cleaning takes a long time. If the pollution is coming from past incarnations, it stays there longer and eventually, in one of your lives, creates dire diseases or very bad social and family conditions. Whenever you can, clean these things. Get rid of them. It takes time, and we are going to try again and again. You can do it also in your home until you see yourself truly transparent, and then you will see, in one week's time, two month's time, that energies are flowing through you.

There is a danger that when you find yourself clean and energetic, you may start abusing yourself. Do not do that. Just keep the energy within you so that you use it in the future.

Q & A

Question: What do you mean by abusing yourself?

Answer: For example, let us say that I have this man here and I tell him he is going to stay celibate for one month and do these exercises. After he does every exercise and he becomes clean, he starts to be so active sexually that he starts to waste his energy in intercourse. He goes after this girl or that girl. He messes himself up. When the energy increases, it is a sign that you must use that energy intelligently, not abuse it and waste it.

You should do this exercise for no more than five minutes. The effectiveness depends on your intensity and the energy you put behind it, or the sincerity of your mind and the motivation that you really want to get rid of your mess. Sometimes I have the experience of wanting to clean this or that vice from my nature. Inside of me I do not really want this, but I do an exercise to clean it and then create a mess inside. You must really want to clean it and get rid of it; you must be completely in it, wanting to become totally clean and beautiful, pure. It depends on your motivation and the energy that you put behind it and also on the level of your consciousness. For example, if you are a conscious being, you put into this exercise five hundred tons of energy. If you are half-conscious, you put half a pound. How much energy are you putting behind it, and how consciously are you doing it; how much are you in it?

A time comes when I am doing these exercises that I become totally in it. I do not know any more that I have a physical body; I do not know where I am. I am just in the exercise. If you do it this way, be totally in it, then the time element is much less. For example, it takes five days, six days, five months, five years, five incarnations. But whatever you do, to whatever degree you do it, it is nice for you because it is money in your bank. You are putting in the bank five dollars, five dollars, five dollars, and three hundred sixty-five days later you have lots of money. On the other hand, if you put in one thousand dollars daily, you will have seven thousand dollars in one week. It depends on you, on your consciousness, your motivation, your sincerity, on the pressure you put behind it, the energy you put behind it, but, no matter to what degree you do it, it is a benefit for you because it going into your bank account.

Question: I found it hard to see the waterfall as very powerful and at the same time imagine that that powerful waterfall was love-compassion. How do you make that powerful waterfall love-compassion?

Answer: Use your visualization or creative imagination. Be patient. Mentally you are going to visualize certain circumstances in which you have exactly what you want. If they are not agreeing, there is a resistance against that within you. Against love, against compassion, there is a resistance. That resistance — who knows how it came into being or how it is coming into being — that resistance can be overcome by doing the exercise again and again.

The water itself is the love and compassion. Compassion is pouring into you. Love is pouring into you. You cannot see the power. The water that is falling drop by drop is love, is blessings, is sweetness — so nice. You are going to feel the water. Creative imagination and visualization change the chemistry of the energy. This is such an important rule. Your visualization changes the chemistry of it. If the chemistry is light, you make whatever you are visualizing become light. Then you change it into love, into power, into beauty. The chemistry changes through your visualization.

Question: *I found myself changing the quality of the water to become almost silent and very still. Is that okay to do?*

Answer: You must realize that if these exercises were very easy to do, tomorrow all of us would be Masters. Your karma does not tolerate that. Even your body does not tolerate that. It needs time to adjust itself, slowly, slowly. We are accelerating the process a little by using willpower and consciousness and destroying all those hindrances and obstacles that are created between us and our bodies so that we can directly influence our bodies. If we leave things up to Nature, Nature will take two thousand years to build a hill. We, on the other hand, can bring in two or three bulldozers and build a hill in a shorter period of time.

We can accelerate the process of purification, and that is what initiation is. The Master Tibetan says that initiations are artificially created. They are not natural. That is why every initiation requires lots of energy and suffering to get there. We accelerate our own evolution. We speed the development of the human being because of the need. The degeneration is so great that we need people to be ready to meet that need.

You are going to change the quality of the water but change only the things that I say. You are going to make it love. First it is water cleansing your physical body, but the deepest cleansing process is taken from the love. Love cleanses and purifies everything. Love is fiery energy and water is hydrogen and oxygen. It is fire, a cleansing process. You are going to think that it is love, love that is falling and cleaning you. It is not easy to explain. I can explain it, but you need to do it.

We cannot do it except by doing it. How do we learn to write A B C D? We do it, and do it, and eventually, we master it.

We are going to bring in the experience of love through our past experiences. What is love? It is as if someone kissed me for the first time, and I was in heaven — that is physical. We are talking about a little more love. What I said is this: The love energy sticks to the things and cleans them. Think about that.

Question: What if we cannot visualize?

Answer: Visualization is really seeing it, like a movie, or as if you were watching television. That is visualization. But if visualization is not achieved, creative imagination does it. That is as powerful as visualization.

Question: You said that if you could not get the black patch to fade you could surgically remove it. I tried that and it was wonderful but I had a feeling that it could come back.

Answer: That is your fear. Think that it will **not** come back. You must clean the fear. Once you do that, it is gone. Christ said something the entire Christian religion misunderstood. He said, "Whatever you bind on the earth, it will be bound in heaven." He told us that everybody has power, authority, to do anything they want for themselves. His followers misunderstood. They totally distorted what He said. He meant that whatever you think in your heart, that is what you are going to become, and whatever you do on earth, you simultaneously do in heaven or in your subtle bodies. In life, time and space do not exist, but people do not realize that. All that you have done has been done everywhere at the same time. Think about it.

Question: I have to imagine myself being on the beach and then seeing myself someplace away

and then my whole body goes sil-
ver and see-through, right?

Answer: Right. It has the same arms, same everything, but it is more subtle and electrical.

I told you from the beginning, do not think that you are going to do it one hundred percent. But if you do it three percent, you are three hundred miles ahead in your evolution. You must start somewhere.

What I wanted thirty or forty years ago when I came here was money. I said, "God give me money." He asked, "What are you going to do?" I said, "I am going to build a university and take the people there three months or three years, cook them, bake them, and throw them out. They will be magnificent fires in the Universe." But maybe because of my unreadiness I could only do so much. But, I am still young!

If you have two, three, five, fifteen million dollars, let us build that university. Then I will not let you go home. You will stay there, day and night doing these exercises. Immediately after two or three months you will see that you are a totally different human being. People are spending two hundred seventy-five billion dollars to build a bomber. Can you imagine that? Give me half of it and to hell with that bomber! Then I will clean the whole world.

God would send a messenger who would say, "Take this," and it would be fifty million dollars. What will I do with it? I will not go to Las Vegas. I will build for you a place that is paradise. We will even have cooks who cook for you, people to massage you, wash you, make everything possible for you so that in three, four, five months you will be in paradise and experience a true transformation.

This exercise, if you do it three, four, five days, three to five months, will totally change you. You are the result of your thoughts. You have a chance here now for two or three hours. Thank God you are so lucky.

Question: I wanted to know about the length of time. Will we know internally?

Answer: These exercises are so harmless. It is just like eating salad. It is fantastic. There is nothing that hurts you, except there are a few things you must not do. Do not take any hallucinogenic drug; do not drink liquor when you do these exercises; and do not do these exercises after sexual intercourse.

Question: You were talking about the waterfall and love-compassion. Are these two different things?

Answer: No, no. Love and compassion are the water itself. You are going to eventually turn your mental machine in such a way that you think that it is not water. It is blessings; it is love that is coming. That is the shift of the mind. Your mind is crystallized in such a way that whatever it has learned, it cannot change. Eventually you are going to say to the mind, "Whatever I want you to present to me, that is what you are going to present . . . . This is an apple." The mind says, "That is an apple." Then you say, "This is a jewel." "No, it is an apple." "No, I am telling you this is a jewel." After a while the mind will say, "This is a jewel," because your mind is going to obey you. If you obey your mind, there will be no change for you. You will be the same cabbage that you were. Unfortunately we have not learned these things. Now you have a chance to learn and to practice it.

Question: If we change our mind and say the water is love, is it one energy and does our mind change it to love-compassion, or does love-compassion come to us?

Answer: The visualization that you see as falling water turns into love energy. The chemistry totally changes, and that is because of our thinking. Why is this microphone wire different from my hair? It is because its frequency is different from that of my hair. If the frequency is the same, both will be the same. With your thought you are changing the frequency of the elements. Water is really love now; it is not water. Fairy tales are so beautiful. Read them and see how in the fairy tales suddenly the horse changes into a bird and flies.

Question: While we are doing this creative imagination, do we have to go somewhere where there is a

waterfall or can we do it inside our head?

Answer: Anywhere. Everything is inside your head. If I say this, you will think I am weird. There is nothing outside of us. Everything is inside. You are seeing things outside because you think you are inside your body.

Question: Do we do these exercises indefinitely?

Answer: Do you eat indefinitely? There is escape in your thoughts — that you must do it, finish it, and escape. Then what are you going to do the rest of the time?

One day I was shaving — quick, quick, quick. Then I came to my senses. Why am I in a hurry? Something was urging me — finish, finish, finish. Do the exercises as it is necessary, but because the amount of pollution that we have and receive is so great, we must resist the pollution by doing the exercises continually.

Question: The past pollution that we are working on — when we can visualize that gone, then we work on other things?

Answer: Yes. If it is gone, it is gone. If something is not gone from your body, you feel it, you see it, you sense it. For example, if you see it, it is better. Here you are exactly seeing in the movie that this is your back. You are rubbing, cleaning, something is sticking. You pour water, wash, and see that finally it is gone. It is totally gone. In the future, fifty million years later, if you were going to have cancer, you are not going to have cancer because you cleaned it now.

I was in Jerusalem and I was practicing these exercises. There was a girl in whom they found cancer cells. She visualized for one week that her bodies are being cleaned. Then she went to the doctor and he did not find any cancer there. It is so powerful, but she was doing the exercises in the best way possible.

Question: What is a piece of transparent shell inside the astral body?

Answer: You are cleaning something that is sticky there. Our astral body has lots of sticky things upon it. For example, feelings of other people, feelings of our husband, wife; even feelings from past lives are still attached to our astral body. We must clean all of them.

Question: What if you cut part of it out?

Answer: Immediately when you cut into it, the body comes and repairs itself. It is just like water. For example, you have a bucket of water and I take one cup away and the water fills in. The astral body is like water. You cannot create wounds in it by cutting it in your visualization.

Question: If you imagine, you really believe that it goes away. Is it true to say it indeed does go away?

Answer: Yes, it does. Even though imagination is not as

powerful as visualization, it is still good.

Question: What happens if your astral body does not want to go back into the physical body?

Answer: You imagine that it is going in. If you pay attention, Nature gives so many keys to us, keys to the things that we want. The first time my Teacher gave me an exercise to show me how to leave my body, stand away from my body, and look at my body, no matter what he did, I did not go out. I was scared. Then he said, "Make up something." So I imagined that I was a horse and my body was a stable. Then the horse jumped out from the stable. Once the horse had jumped out, I changed back into myself and looked at my body.

It is tricky. You will keep trying until you are out of your body. Sooner or later you are going to learn it, but realize that we are five million years late in our evolution because the Satan of the world — materialism — got us. Materialism, hatred, wars, jealousy, and revenge are occupying eighty percent of everyone's time and money. We do not have time to think about these fantastic things. Twenty-three hours you are working for your body. Imagine that. If you do five minutes meditation, you think it is too much, that you are doing God a favor!

Exercise 4

Purification of the Mental Body

— Now rest. Be happy. Relax your body and relax your face and imagine you are in paradise. Do not think about your faults, mistakes, and so on. That is all past. Let it go to hell. You can sit back on your chair because there is no center involved in this. Make your face very relaxed, especially your eyeballs and your eyebrows.

— Now go to the waterfall again and do not enter. There is a subtle thing here. Put your physical body on the sand and look at it as if you are the astral body. Then set your astral body beside it and look at both of them. One is the physical body, the other is the transparent astral body, the jellyfish. Touch them and see how they feel. They are so similar, each just a copy of the other, only one is silvery, transparent, translucent. See if you can find some dirt, some pollution in the astral body and say, "Later I will clean you."

— Now visualize you are the lemon yellow mental body. You no longer have the form of the physical body. Now you are a ball of light. You are a ball of lemon yellow light. You need a change in consciousness here now. You do not have hands, but you have two big eyes — you, the lemon yellow sphere of energy. You are a sphere of light, but on that sphere there are patches of dirt. What are they?

> • One is called **ego.** It is a painful wound, and whenever anyone touches that wound you

scream very loudly.
- The next one is **vanity**. You think that you are somebody, something.
- The next pollution is **greed**. It is like a sucking worm — that is greed.
- And then there is a crystallized wound there which is called **fanaticism**. It is a very hardened patch in the mental body.
- There are also some zigzag energies cutting each other. These belong to the sickness called **separatism.**

And there you have five very important, very significant pollutants.

— Now enter into the waterfall, which this time is a current of yellow electricity. It is pouring and cleaning you, inside, outside. Try to get rid of pollutants, of these five kinds of diseases in your mental body. I will repeat: They are **ego, vanity, fanaticism, separatism**, and **greed**. Now put that yellow sphere — you — under the water and let the water clean it. It is all electrical water and when it hits your mental body, it slowly, slowly wipes away these ailments.

— Start your exercise now. Keep yourself awake. Do not sleep. Clean it, clean it, relax, relax. Do not force it. It will go by itself. When your hands are muddy, you put them under the water and the mud goes. In the same way, do not force this. The mental body cannot be forced.

Just let it flow, that fiery, electrical energy which is pouring into all of your mental body.

— Now, while you are under the shower, let that sphere of energy open and see at the middle of it a Chalice. Let energy hit it and see a blue light coming out of the Chalice. Let it radiate out.

— Now you see blue energy radiated from the center of that yellow sphere, and it is so beautiful. You are under the shower. Call your astral body and dress in it. You are still in the shower. Call your physical body, dress in it, and now you are under the shower and all bodies are integrated and cleaned and beautiful. Play with the waterfall and enjoy it for five minutes. Do anything you want. You have your physical body, astral body, and mental body. Sing a very nice song, thanking God. Express gratitude for the fact that you are clean physically, emotionally, mentally. You are together, fantastic, and so let it be.

— Take your time for a few minutes now and enjoy yourself under the waterfall, doing whatever you would like to do. Keep yourself under the waterfall. Your three bodies are receiving the energy simultaneously. Jump and swim a little. Now slowly, slowly get out, sit on a rock there. Now visualize yourself sitting on your chair and think about your room. Rub your hands. Rub your face. Slowly open your eyes.

Q & A

Question: What does it mean when you just go away, but do not necessarily fall asleep?

Answer: That either you should not do it because you are tired or else you relaxed too much. We must be relaxed but keep our consciousness awake. The physical body must sleep, the consciousness must be awake. That is what you are going to do. As I said, these exercises are just the beginning. If we continue this, month after month, year after year, in a few months' time, in a few years' time, you will see that you are a totally different human being. We did these exercises once in the monastery for six months. After six months I was walking in the clouds; I was totally different — dynamite. The earth, the life that we are living, is eating us. The general life is eating us. We are wasting our time and energy intended for the real work. We are not in our spiritual being yet. Eventually it will come, doing these things. Slowly, slowly, step-by-step, we will reach our independence, our freedom.

Question: What happens to the mental thoughtforms when you do this?

Answer: They totally dissolve and go away. A moment came that I did not know who I was. I forgot my name because actually I do not have a name. A name is just for practical reasons, a label. They are putting the label on the bottle and saying, "This is Lou." Who said that bottle is Lou? Take the bottle away and there is no Lou.

As I said, I forgot my name. Then I adapted myself, slowly, slowly. All you are is spirit. You do not have names, ages. How old are you? Sixty years old. You are talking about your body.

We build physical, emotional, and mental bodies and then we build higher bodies. Then the most important thing is that these two bodies engage themselves in such a way that you are earthly, but you are heavenly at the same time. You are heavenly but also earthly. There must be no gap in your consciousness.

Some people, especially in the sixties, hippy-zippies, were like balloons floating in the sky. They did not have any practical life, any food or necessities. They were floating. We do not want to float. We want to be awake on both sides of our existence, balanced. You will be a very advanced Master, but in the meantime you will be able to play with a child or go play football and enjoy your friends without any vanity . . . because you are balanced.

Question: In the final waterfall when our bodies are together, what is the nature of the waterfall?

Answer: It is three things: body, emotions, and mind, three energies united together. You will understand more if you start doing these exercises daily or weekly for five minutes. You will see one month later, two months later that you feel so dynamic because weakness of the bodies is the result of pollution in your bodies. Medical science calls these pollutants by lots of names: microbes, viruses, germs, bugs, crazy names — Roman, Greek, and so on. They are all pollution, nothing else. Wipe them out.

Through visualization you direct energy and you change the nature of energy. Your mind is a great alchemist. It is a magician. It can do things that seem impossible for an average man. Five hundred years later you will have built a bridge by your visualization and will travel upon it.

CHAPTER FOUR

Organization

Exercise 1

AUM
FIRST SERIES

1. Visualize your three bodies:
   physical
   emotional
   mental
2. Sound the AUM seven times, each time charging the physical body with a violet energy.
3. Sound the AUM seven times, each time charging the emotional body with silvery energy.
4. Sound the AUM seven times, each time charging the mental body with yellow energy.
   - Take your time. Concentrate your attention every time you are sounding the AUM.
   - Then you have, as a whole, seven AUMs for each body and twenty-one total for the three bodies.
   - When beginning, visualize your physical body, and

make the seven AUMs really penetrate every cell of your body.

• Then recollect yourself for a few seconds and visualize your astral body and sound seven AUMs, making the silvery energy penetrate into the astral body each time.

• Then recollect yourself for a few seconds and visualize your mental body and sound seven AUMs, each time making the yellow energy of the AUM penetrate into your mental body.

Then, rest for five minutes.

Exercise 2

AUM
SECOND SERIES

When you have done the first series correctly for 15 days, then you can sound the AUM in a little different manner.

— The first seven AUMs directed to the physical body will be used in the following way:

> A - violet
> U - silver
> M - lemon yellow
> Repeat seven times for the physical body.

— Send the second AUM to the astral body in the following way:

> A - violet
> U - silver
> M - lemon yellow
> Repeat this seven times.

— Send the third AUM to the mental body in the following way:

> A - violet
> U - silver
> M - lemon yellow
> Repeat this seven times.
> Try with every letter (A-U-M) to direct the colors.

Exercise 3

AUM
Third Series

Now in this next hour we are going to do exercises with sound, or with the Sacred Word. These are powerful exercises for integration and wholeness.

— You are going to sound in your mind twenty-one AUMs mentally. Suppose I am doing it mentally, just in this way. Seven to the physical, seven to the astral, and seven to the mental bodies:

AAAAAAAUUUUUUUMMMMMMM

That was one AUM.

— Now you are going to send

    1. seven AUMs to your physical body, visualizing violet energy
    2. seven AUMs to your emotional body, visualizing silvery energy
    3. seven AUMs to your mental body, visualizing lemon yellow energy

— Each time you are sounding the AUM, see the electrical energy going to all of your body, integrating it and making it whole.

— Let me repeat the colors. For the physical body, imagine the color violet. See how violet energy is hitting your physical body, penetrating every cell, every bone, every organ — but do it slowly. Sound the first AUM. Wait and imagine, visualize. Then, do the emotional body in silvery color, and the mental body in lemon yellow.

— Imagine in slow motion, but mentally do it as if you were shouting.

— Now we are starting, seven of them. Go slowly and visualize. Start. Between them you have a few seconds to visualize until it reaches your toes, everywhere.

— You are going too fast. Go slower, like this . . . AAAUUUMMM and then visualize that every place is filled. Okay.

— It has to go throughout the whole body each time, or else you create imbalance in your system. AUM is going all over. There are three kinds of energy that must balance it.

Q & A

Question: Are you in your body when you are doing it?

Answer: Actually you are never in your physical body, but you feel as if you were.

Question: When you sound the AUM, do you see something coming from somewhere?

Answer. Just visualize that through the sound of the AUM you are charging your physical body with violet energy. Sound AAAAAAA starting with violet energy, UUUUUUU penetrating all your bones, hands, nails, hair, MMMMMMM in your nose, toes, everything.

Question: Do we break with each syllable?

Answer: There is no stop. AAAAAAAUUUUUUUMMMMMMM.

Question: Do we do the first set for the physical, the second set for the emotional?

Answer: Yes, each body receives a set of seven AUMs, in that order: physical is violet energy, emotional is silvery energy, mental is lemon yellow energy.

Question: You did say we do it silently?

Answer: Yes. You are going to sit nicely and take a nice breath and do the first AUM. Your visualization is going to direct the energy. If you do not visualize that the violet energy is going to your bones, toes, nose, hair, ears, and inner organs, it does not go. You are going to direct that energy with your willpower and concentration. AUM is energy. Now the first time it is violet energy. That violet energy is penetrating every part of your body. Do not direct that energy into any special place, only to the whole body.

Question: Is there a way to regulate the AUM with your breathing?

Answer: Yes, but because you are doing it mentally you can breathe differently. For example, if you are breathing twice with the lungs, mentally breathe four times, with a four-to-one ratio.

Exercise 4

AUM
FOURTH SERIES

Now let us pass to the next series of AUM. The following diagram will make it easier for you to understand:

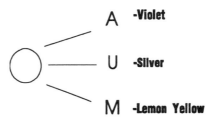

Repeat seven times—Physical Body

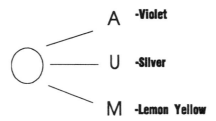

Repeat seven times—Emotional Body

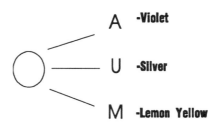

Repeat seven times—Mental Body

Now we have these three:

A - violet energy

U - silver energy

M - Yellow energy

Let us say that the physical, astral, and mental bodies each contains physical, emotional, and mental substances. The physical body, for example, is not only physical but also part emotional, part mental. It is the same for the astral and mental bodies. This is only the AUM for this round, and it is divided into three colors for each.

Now, let us start this round. "A" is violet; "U" is silver; "M" is lemon yellow. That is it. Finish seven such AUMs for one body and pass to the next body.

Look what is happening. If you are an artist you will understand. See the diagram. The physical body is violet, the astral body is silver, and the mental body is lemon yellow. Now you are mixing three energies: violet, silver, and yellow. For the physical body violet is predominant, for the astral body silver is predominant, and for the mental body lemon yellow is predominant.

Each body will receive seven AUMs, with three colors, seven times. One AUM is divided into three. I am going to give you ten minutes to do it. Do not go too fast, nor too slow. The main thing is that you spread the colors totally throughout your body. The first seven go totally throughout your physical body.

Try to think that all cells, organs, glands — all elements — are receiving the three energies, not only violet but also silver and yellow.

Then, visualize your astral body. Again AUM, three energies, seven times.

Then do the mental. When you come to the end of ten minutes, you must be finished and sitting quietly.

The first color is always violet. The "A" is always violet, no matter what body it is in. "U" is always silver and "M" is always yellow in whichever case. No matter what body you are in, it follows that sequence.

You start with the physical body. Relax. Take a nice breath, one more, one more. Now start at your own pace. You have ten minutes. Okay, be here now.

Q & A

Question: When you do that last exercise, are you in each of the separate bodies or are you watching the separate bodies? Can you feel you are that particular body?

Answer: It depends on what your evolution is, but the most important thing is to send these three energies each time: AUM to one body, AUM to the second body, AUM to the third body, each time with three colors. The difficulty for most of you is that you are not differentiating the colors very well. For example, you should see your physical as violet. Start with violet, go to silver, go to yellow.

Then you visualize your emotional body as silver. Go to violet, silver, then yellow.

Then you visualize your mental body as yellow. Go to violet, silver, and yellow. Three times seven you integrated with the three; nine, you integrated all the three bodies together.

I recommend that individually you do these exercises early in the morning until you learn firsthand what happens. Experience it. If you are ready for it, you must do this every day until the end of your life, before or after meditation, but always in the morning. The whole thing takes five, six minutes. Five minutes to invest for your life is nothing, but people do not do it. You will see that each day you do the exercise, that day you will be totally different, physically, emotionally, mentally. Then, one, two, three years later your physical, emotional, and mental bodies will not impose themselves upon you. Instead, they will obey.

Question: On the last three AUMs, are we doing three colors?

Answer: Yes, it is each body, three colors. That is why I said nine. It is three bodies, three colors. Three times three is nine.

Sounding the AUM this way is a cleansing, purifying experience. There are lots of impurities in our system. Even if you have been very holy-poly in this life, you can bring out lots of trash from past lives. We have to clean all that.

People have been told that karma cannot be cleaned, but that is not true. The Great Sage says something very important about this, that willpower and thought clean karma. Our debts are paid and finished.

Question: How does thinking clean the karma?

Answer: It is because through thinking you can destroy the causes of the karma. If there is a nest within your mind that totally produces the seed of lies, and through your thought you destroy that nest and you do not lie anymore, it is finished — no more lying. The causes must be eliminated. When the causes are eliminated, the effects will be eliminated. Who has read the chapter on evening review in *The Psyche and Psychism*?

Did you read there the idea that if you do evening review, you destroy your karma? That is why Christ said something, "If you fight with your friend now, before sunset you need to go and clean your account with him. Forgive each other and finish it." Especially a wife and husband must not go to sleep with anger after sunset. It will be cleared. It does not go in your book. Then karma is not registered.

Question: When you clean a spot, do you have to know what that was?

Answer: No, you do not need to know. I can give exercises and clean it, and everything is cleaned wholesale so that you do not know what you cleaned. For example, if there is a spot on your wall, you do not take the microscope and ask, "What is this?" You clean it and finish it. Who cares what it is?

These are conditioning exercises. Conditioning has a totally different philosophical meaning than you think. Conditioning means that you come to expect different results in the future from what you are doing now. We call it conditioning. You are conditioning yourself, and you will feel better and better and your health will be better and better. But do not exaggerate, and, if you have any problem at all, ask me.

Question: Is it also better for a couple to meditate together?

Answer: Yes. That means a group. A group is more than

one person; more than one person is always a group. Actually three people are better, but two people are good because two people are four people: two people and their Solar Angels, and if God is present there it will be five!

Question: What is the goal of this last exercise?

Answer: The goal is to purify and exercise your whole personality and align it with your Soul. You feel integrated, together.

Question: Is it practical to do the AUM out loud?

Answer: If you are alone you can do that; also, if you are two or three people. As a group you must do it on the same note. It is best if you sound the AUM using F sharp.

CHAPTER FIVE

Radiation

Exercise

The Self

1. Relax for a few minutes.
2. Focus your consciousness in the middle of your head.
3. Think about your body. Realize that some day it is going to die and disappear.
4. Think about your emotional nature and realize that it too, in due time, will melt away into the corresponding reservoir of Nature.
5. Think about your mental mechanism. See what it can do or is doing. Consider it as a machine or a tool you are using and with which you are often closely identified. Realize that it is a temporary, a finite tool which can be used for various purposes.
6. Visualize yourself as being the living Self within these three natures. Step out and think as if you were a part of the Self of the Universe.

7. Think that the One Self is in every form, in all space, in all stars and heavenly constellations. Think that that Self is everywhere uniting all forms that exist on globes and in space.

8. Think that you are that Self, everywhere and in everything. Think that your consciousness in time will expand to such a degree that it will embrace the whole that exists in the Self. Think that nothing exists apart from the Self.

9. Think about billions of stars and realize that you are everywhere, being a part of that Self, of that all-pervading Self.

10. Feel the joy, the bliss, that your soul senses in such an awareness, an awareness of freedom, the freedom of Infinity, total contentment.

11. After reaffirming such an awareness, turn back and enter into your mental, astral, and physical bodies, and feel that you are a person, but with the awareness of the One Self.

12. Now think about your duties, responsibilities, and relationships with your family, group, society, and nation; with other kingdoms; and with humanity as a whole.

13. Think what the quality of your action or labor in the world will be, having been blessed by the consciousness of the One Self.

What will be your emotional relations with others while breathing and living in the consciousness of the One Self?

What will be the nature of your words, conversations, lectures? What will be the quality and aim of your creativity? How will you use your personality and for what purpose?

Thus the realization of the One Self may shift the axis on which all your deeds, emotions, thoughts, and speech lie, and challenge you to have a new approach to life, an approach which is conditioned by your awareness of the One Self.

14. At this stage you can think and contemplate your future self-image and think practically about the changes you are going to introduce into your life and relationships.

This is the most important point where your transformation will start, and you will impress your nature to respond to your awareness of Self.

15. After you go through such an exercise or discipline for thirty minutes to one hour, your other duty will be to increase your observation of your thoughts, emotions, words, and actions so that you do not let your lower nature or personality act against the Law of the One Self or against your awareness of the One Self. This will be great fun and a source of experience about your true psychology and level of beingness.

We suggest that for a few years you do this exercise only once a week, and then only when you can retreat and focus yourself on such a task. After two or three years you can do it for thirty minutes, twice a week, and then continue this to the last day of your life on this earth.

The effect of such a discipline will be highly beneficial:

1. Your health will improve.
2. You will be more successful in your work.
3. New and higher help will reach you to meet your needs.
4. Your magnetism will increase and many visible and invisible co-workers will gather around you.
5. You will have supermundane contacts.
6. You will feel secure, protected, fearless, and free.
7. Your life will turn into a service for humanity.

CHAPTER SIX

Creativity

Exercise 1

Recreating Yourself

This exercise is a fantastic one, and if it is done properly it may call out all your creative energies into action.

— Relax. Close your eyes and through your visualization create a new image of yourself, a new personality.

— Do not pay attention to any opposing image from the past. Think that you can recreate yourself. You have that power within you, and often, when the opposition is great, your creative power becomes stronger.

— Create a new image for yourself.

— What kind of body do you want? What kind of face do you want? What kind of hair do you want? What kind of mannerisms do you want? How and with what voice do you want to speak? How do you want to smile?

You can recreate your self-image. How do you want to walk? How do you want to listen? How do you want your hand and face movements to be?

Create an image that you want. For one week, two weeks, two months, work for a new image, and see how your thoughts and emotions are assisting you to have that new self-image.

You can do this when you are alone for fifteen, twenty minutes. Be particular. Go slowly. Do not jump from one part to another part of your self-image. Whatever you do, do it with perfection, in every way a little better than before. You will be amazed how various etheric, emotional, and mental forces will assist you to change your self-image.

Daily try to live as if your self-image were changing and influencing people in a new way. People are feeling and seeing the change in you.

— After you do this exercise for three to six months, take the next creative exercise and work on it another three to six months.

I have seen artists working two to four years on their paintings, drawings, sculptures, carvings, but the best creativity is self-creativity. You must recreate yourself. This is the greatest honor for yourself. This is the greatest help for yourself. This is the greatest help for yourself on the path of your spiritual evolution.

Exercise 2

Recreating Your Labor

1. Daily retreat for twenty, thirty minutes and recreate your present labor or create a new labor.

Let us take your routine labor and try to visualize doing these things:

      a) improving it

      b) expanding it

      c) making it a true service for humanity

      d) making it a true service for the Plan of the Great Ones

Then you will put into action those energies which will make your wishes and plans come true.

You will be surprised that as your labor increases and expands, you will also go through creative changes. New talents, new inspiration, new faculties will emerge from within you and enable you to cope with the expansion of your labor.

This is a fantastic method to make you successful, but you must go "slow but sure" in your visualization process. You must see the changing of your entire laboring effort: the employees, the way they work, and the entire relationship of your labor with the world.

Do not hurry. See every day as if you were changing your labor into a better, bigger labor. Go step-by-step. Whatever your labor is it does not matter. Try to improve and perfect it. Visualize how you are practically improving it. Take all phases of your labor. Never leave any phase of it untouched. See how your new self-image is working as you recreate your labor, making it new.

If you want to change the form of your labor, then you are going to visualize an entirely new labor, and start building it in detail, step-by-step from the beginning, bringing it to the level you want to reach.

The creation of life needs visualization, willpower — or a strong desire or recognition of need and willingness to meet that need — continuous improvement, and expansion.

2. Create a new office.

You have an office, a place in which you operate your business, your work, your labor. Whatever, wherever it is, now visualize an ideal office, equipped to render the best service for you.

a) desk — Improve or recreate it daily.

b) file cabinets — Put them in order so as not to lose time searching for documents.

c) machines — Keep them in an operating state.

d) chairs, other objects — Try to arrange them in a way that they do not hinder the operation of your business.

Make everything clean and up-to-date.

Of course you need money, space, assistants, but all these you will acquire through your visualization.

When the thoughtform of your new office is built and changed by your visualization, you will be surprised how one day the objective change will occur, manifesting all that you visualized.

Visualization builds the prototype, and the materialization of the prototype soon actualizes in your life at just the right time. Do not worry about the materialization of your visualization. The only thing you must do is to visualize as if you already have all the facilities under control. The rest is in the hands of the energies and laws of the Universe.

3. Create a new group of students, workers, friends, servers to promote your plan for helping humanity in any way you wish.

To create a group around you takes the patient labor of visualization. Choose the individuals. Visualize those characteristics that you want them to have. Create rules for their group formation. Give them labor of any kind (study, compilation, construction, teaching). See them doing their labor in better and better ways. See your group becoming a powerful, influential group in the world. See the members lecturing, writing, publishing, singing, playing music. See them influencing the public consciousness.

Equip them with the most recent machinery, computers, faxes, CD-ROMs, dictionaries, and other necessary equipment. See them attracting publishing and distributing companies.

Go slowly. Do not daydream, but make it real, practical, so that the whole prototype is built with perfect engineering, like a whole building built properly to serve the purpose.

Realize that your future group will be exactly what you demanded from the Universe through your visualization. "Ask and it will be given to you," said the Great Lord.

Visualization is an act of asking in the mental plane, a powerful way of asking. Do this for six months, twenty to thirty minutes daily.

Sometimes your monkey emotions will say, "Do not waste your time. You have television; you have a dinner party; you have visitors; you have swimming; you have to go . . . . All this rubbish may distract you. Tell your monkey mind that you have the determination to be somebody, that you are going to be that which you want to be.

Even your karma cannot stand in your way. It will be an illegal act to stand in your way. Your karma can cause some hindrances, difficulties to be sure, but once you show your determination, it assists you.

Karma wants you to crush your obstacles and emerge victorious in your life.

Exercise 3

Health and Happiness

Use your visualization for your health and happiness.

— Daily for six months visualize for thirty minutes that you are going to be the most healthy person. Visualize your body, organs, glands as a whole, and think how they are improving in their operation, in their function. See them revitalized, energized, perfect.

— See your lymph system cleansing all trash from your body. Visualize your blood destroying all hostile elements. See all your organs in perfect shape. See the energy of life circulating throughout your body, emotions, and mind.

— Visualize your body having perfect balance with Cosmic energies. Dedicate your body, your health, to the service of God's Plan, to the service of humanity.

— Visualize yourself walking, running, swimming, and dancing in the best health and energy. If this is done right, you will put into action all the regenerative energies in Nature to make you a dynamic, powerful, and healthy individual whose sole purpose is to have the joy of serving humanity.

— Visualize yourself walking in radiant health and energy.

Read the books *New Dimensions in Healing* and *Sex, Family, and the Woman in Society.* These books will assist you to have better visualization for your health.

CHAPTER SEVEN

Presence

Exercises

On Presence

This is to make you aware that you are all-visible and watched, and will evoke from you certain states of consciousness which can be very constructive and creative.

1. Visualize yourself in the presence of your Solar Angel, Who is a fiery being, a Nirvani from other schemes or solar systems. Imagine Him as an "Initiate of all degrees," as the Tibetan Master puts it. Increase your information about the Solar Angel by reading our publication, *The Solar Angel*.

   It is very vital that through your visualization process you create a real, direct contact with Him. Visualize Him in a form that pleases you and stand in His presence not only by visualizing yourself in His presence but also by visualizing yourself as doing anything you want in His presence. You may even converse with Him, wonder at

His glory, know about His private life, know His expectations for you, and so on. This visualization will not be emotional or done on the astral plane, because in this plane many entities masquerade as Him and approach you as your Solar Angel. That is why, before you start your visualization, you must focus your consciousness in your higher mind and be always in the state of reasoning and logic. You may experience a few attempts of attack from lower entities, but you can soon repel them as your experience deepens. Most of the time your Solar Angel repels such entities.

Do this for four months. Make your Solar Angel real in your life. In your physical, emotional, and mental relationships see His life guiding you. Very soon you will see a great difference between your past and present.

You will feel uplifted into a new state of consciousness and be able to see the life you were living in the past as being trapped in vices and problems, wasting your life in purposeless activities. After a few months, proceed with the second step in the Exercise of Presence.

2. Be in the presence of your Master on the path. See who He is, what He expects from you, how close you are to Him. This is a fantastic visualization discipline which builds a path of contact between you and your real Master living in this world.

Visualize talking with Him, living and acting in His presence. Try to find the difference between Him and your Solar Angel. Do this every day for four months until His presence in your life becomes a reality. Note in your diary if you have had any experience with Him.

Here also many dark ones can interfere and present themselves as your Master. Use your discrimination. Read *Letters on Occult Meditation* and *The Externalisation of the Hierarchy* to have more information about the Master. Read also *Supermundane*.

3. Visualize yourself attending Ashrams where a Great One is teaching. Every day visualize attending and listening to the lectures or instructions. Learn what an Ashram is and how it functions. Use your visualization.

At the beginning you may have difficulty in visualizing any talk or instruction given in the Ashram, but if you continue your exercises of visualization, you will overcome the difficulty. One day you will even feel that you were in an Ashram, and you will remember a few sentences from the Ashram.

Remember, you can make anything real through your visualization. Have faith in your visualization.

4. Visualize yourself working with the Hierarchy, working in the Hierarchy. This is a supreme way to transform all your life and to create fundamental changes in your character.

I will let you do this according to your choice and state of consciousness. Remember only that you need to know more about the Hierarchy, and the best books to study are *Initiation, Human and Solar*; *The Externalisation of the Hierarchy*; and *Supermundane*.

Use your visualization the best way possible, utilizing the information gained from the above mentioned books. Do this exercise twenty minutes daily for five months.

5. Visualize yourself free from your bodies. Here also you must do this the way you want. Read *Other Worlds* and you will have enough information to do this visualization. Do this ten minutes for each body for six months.

6. Visualize yourself traveling from star to star. Create your own plane of existence and visualize the way you think is right.

CHAPTER EIGHT

Summary

You can do these exercises until you pass away. They will heal, uplift, regenerate, strengthen, and enlighten you. All of these exercises lead you toward self-transformation:

1. **Purity** leads to enlightenment.

2. **Organization** leads you to health.

3. **Radiation** develops your will and rejects unwholesome attacks.

4. **Creativity** establishes relationship with other and higher worlds.

5. **Presence** leads into actualization of Beingness.

6. **Freedom** from the bodies destroys the fear of death.

7. **Travel** annihilates the pressure from time and space.

Index

About the Author

This booklet is a transcription of a seminar given by Torkom Saraydarian.

The author's books have been used all over the world as sources of guidance and inspiration for those seeking to live a life based on the teachings of the Ageless Wisdom. Some of the books have been translated into other languages, including Armenian, German, Dutch, Danish, Portuguese, French, Spanish, Italian, Greek, Yugoslavian, and Swedish.

Torkom Saraydarian's entire life has been a zealous effort to help people live healthy, joyous, and successful lives. He has spread this message of love and true vision tirelessly throughout his life. He holds lectures and seminars in the United States as well as in other parts of the world.

From early boyhood the author learned first-hand from teachers of the Ageless Wisdom. He has studied widely in the world's religions and philosophies. In addition, he is an accomplished pianist, violinist, and cellist, and plays many other instruments as well. His books, lectures, seminars, and music are inspiring and offer a true insight into the beauty of the Ageless Wisdom.

Suggested Readings

Saraydarian, Torkom. Cave Creek, AZ: T.S.G. Publishing Foundation, Inc.

Buddha Sutra, A Dialogue with the Glorious One

New Dimensions in Healing

Thought and the Glory of Thinking

Saraydarian, Torkom. Sedona, AZ: Starfire Recordings
Infinity

Saraydarian, Torkom. Sedona, AZ: Aquarian Educational Group.

The Science of Meditation

Sex, Family, and the Woman in Society

The Solar Angel

Agni Yoga Society. New York: Agni Yoga Society.
Supermundane, Vols. I, and II

Bailey, Alice A. New York: Lucis Publishing Co.
Externalisation of the Hierarchy

Initiation Human and Solar

Letters on Occult Meditation

All are available directly through
T.S.G. Publishing Foundation, Inc.
Write or call for details

**Other Books by
Torkom Saraydarian**

Symphony of the Zodiac
Talks on Agni
Triangles of Fire
Unusual Court
Woman, Torch of the Future
The Year 2000 & After

Booklets

A Daily Discipline of Worship
Angels and Devas
Building Family Unity
Cornerstones of Health
Earthquakes and Disasters — What the Ageless Wisdom Tells Us
Fiery Carriage and Drugs
First Steps Toward Freedom
Five Great Mantrams of the New Age
Hierarchy and the Plan
Irritation — The Destructive Fire
Nachiketas
New Beginnings
Practical Spirituality
The Psychology of Cooperation
Questioning Traveler and Karma
Responsibility
Responsibility and Business
The Responsibility of Fathers
The Responsibility of Mothers
Spring of Prosperity
Success
Synthesis
Torchbearers
What to Look for in the Heart of Your Partner

Videos

The Seven Rays Interpreted
Lecture Videos by Author

Ordering Information

Write to the publisher for additional information regarding:

— Free catalog of author's books and music tapes

— Lecture tapes and videos — complete list available

— Placement on mailing list

— New releases

— A free copy of our newsletter Outreach

Price Per Copy: U.S. $6.00

Postage within U.S.A. - $3.00
Plus applicable state sales tax
International postage by Airmail or Surface - Contact us

T.S.G. Publishing Foundation, Inc.
P.O. Box 7068
Cave Creek, AZ 85331-7068
United States of America

T.S.G. Publishing Foundation, Inc.
Complete Line of Torkom Saraydarian's Works
P.O. Box 7068, Cave Creek, AZ 85327 USA
Tel: 480-502-1909 * Fax: 480-502-0713
www.tsgfoundation.org

T.S.G. Publishing Foundation, Inc. is a non-profit, tax-exempt organization.

Our purpose is to be a pathway for self-transformation. We offer books, audio and video tapes, classes and seminars, and home study courses based on the core values and higher principles of the Ageless Wisdom.

These fine books have been published by the generous donations of the students of the Ageless Wisdom.

Your tax deductible contributions will help us continue publishing and growing.

Our gratitude to all.